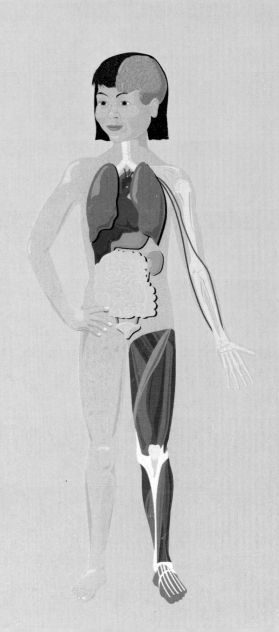

Text: Lesley Newson
Consultant: Dr. Rosemary Evans MB, BS (London), DObst., RCOG, DCH (London), MRCP (UK)
Computer illustrations: Mel Pickering, Graham Smith
Watercolour illustrations: Helen Herbert
Photo research: Liz Eddison

Editorial Directors: Sue Hook, Carolyn Jackson
Art Director: Belinda Webster
Production Director: Lorraine Estelle
Editor: Lucy Duke
Assistant Editors: Mimi George, Samantha Hilton, Deborah Kespert
Co-editions Editors: Mathew Birch, Robert Sved
Assistant Designer: Lisa Nutt

Photo credits: Brian and Cherry Alexander: p26 (top right); Allsport: p27 (bottom left); Anthony Bannister/OSF: p29 (top left); Dr. Jeremy Burgess/Science Photo Library: p69 (top left); Scott Camazine/Science Photo Library: p18 (top left); Tom Campbell/Britstock-IFA: p62 (top); Peter Davey/Bruce Coleman: p81 (bottom right); Nicholas De Vore/Bruce Coleman: p41; Diaf/Britstock-IFA: p59 (bottom); Bernd Ducke/Britstock-IFA: p47 (top); Goedel/Britstock-IFA: p82; Paul Harris/Royal Geographical: p8; The Image Bank: p38 (right) p39, p50 (top right), p59 (top right), p74, p75 (top), p83 (bottom), p86 (bottom left); Images Colour Library: p10-11; Wayne Lankinen/Bruce Coleman: p78 (bottom left); NASA/Science Photo Library: p25; NIBSC/Science Photo Library: p17 (bottom right); The Photographers Library: p33 (bottom right); Pictor International: p9; Neil Ray/Trip: p49; David Scharf/Science Photo Library: p40 (bottom left), p69 (centre left); Sipa/Britstock-IFA: p67 (top right); Tony Stone: p36 (top right), p50 (bottom left), p51 (bottom), p58 (top right), p60 (right), p61 (right); Tektoff/Science Photo Library: p66; Telegraph Colour Library: p30 (top), p37 (top left), p38 (bottom left), p53, p60 (left), p83 (top); Steve Turner/OSF: p71 (bottom right); Jennie Woodcock/Reflections: p21 (bottom right); Zefa: p24 (top right), p27 (bottom right), p43 (top right), p51 (top), p57 (top), p75 (bottom right), p81 (top left), p87 (top right)

Scholastic Children's Books, Scholastic Publications Ltd, 7-9 Pratt Street, London, NW1 0AE, UK

Scholastic Inc., 555 Broadway, New York, NY 10012-3999, USA

Scholastic Canada Ltd, 123 Newkirk Road, Richmond Hill, Ontario, Canada, L4C 3G5

Ashton Scholastic Pty Ltd, PO Box 579, Gosford, New South Wales, Australia

Ashton Scholastic Ltd, Private Bag 92801, Penrose, Auckland, New Zealand

First published in the UK by Scholastic Publications Ltd, 1995
Copyright © 1995 by Scholastic Publications Ltd and Two-Can Publishing Ltd
All rights reserved

A catalogue record for this book is available from the British Library.

ISBN: 0 590 54198 6
ISBN for title set: 0 590 54201 X

2 4 6 8 10 9 7 5 3 1

Printed by Proost in Belgium
Colour reproduction by Daylight Colour Art Pte Ltd, Singapore

All About People

SCHOLASTIC

How to use this book

Look it up!

All About People tells you about yourself and the people around you. The Contents page tells you all the subjects, or entries, discussed in this book and on what page they begin. There are entries on parts of your body, such as Bones, and about how your body works, such as Seeing. Entries are organized in alphabetical order. There are other entries that tell about different times in your life, such as Young children. These are placed throughout the book, and they are in chronological order, starting with Babies and toddlers and ending with Older adults.

Glossary

Words in the book that may be difficult to understand are marked in **bold**. The Glossary near the back of the book lists these words and explains what they mean.

Index

The Index at the back of the book is a list of everything mentioned in the book, arranged in alphabetical order, with its page number. If an entry is in *italics*, it means that it is a label on a diagram.

If the number only is in *italics*, the entry appears in the main text as well as being a diagram.

Cross-references

Above the coloured bar on each page there is a list of other entries in the book or in the other three books in the *Scholastic First Encyclopedia*, with their book titles. These other entries tell you more about the subject on the page.

Pronunciation

Some words, such as encyclopedia (say "en-sy-clo-pee-dee-a"), are difficult to pronounce. To say them correctly, make the sounds in the brackets after each of the words.

Diagrams

Many diagrams in *All About People* show what your body looks like inside. In the diagrams, body parts are brightly coloured, so they are easy to see, even though they may not be this colour inside your body. Each body part is the same colour throughout the book.

Contents

People are special animals

People belong to the group of animals called mammals. Mammals are animals whose babies are born live rather than hatched from eggs. All mammal babies can drink milk from their mother's body. Cats, dogs, horses and whales are mammals. But human beings are different in some important ways.

Most mammals move about on all four feet, but people walk upright. Our hipbones are specially shaped to help us keep our balance. People have thumbs that can grasp things. Unlike other animals, people can survive in many different environments. We can live almost anywhere in the world.

▶ People often keep other animals as pets. If you take good care of your pets, they can be some of your best friends.

Using our brains
People have very well-developed brains. Our brains let us talk to each other in complicated languages. We use our brains to think, learn, invent, build and discover. The human brain can store millions of memories which we use to help us decide how to behave and how we feel.

▲ Some animals, such as dolphins, are very intelligent. But as far as we know, people are the only animals who are aware of their thoughts.

How people are different –

Human beings have many different sizes and shapes. We also have a variety of colours of hair, eyes and skin. No two people are exactly the same. With all the millions of people in the world, there is no one who has the same fingerprints that you do. Even identical twins, who may have the same height and the same hair, eye and skin colour have different fingerprints, thoughts, memories and habits.

All About People shows how the human body works, inside and out. It also tells you about people's feelings, and how we live with each other. Some pages show you how people grow and change throughout a lifetime, from birth to old age.

▶ As you read and look at this book, think about the many ways in which the people you know are the same and the many ways in which each person is different.

and the same

Babies and toddlers

All people start life as babies. You can think of babies as tiny people who are new to the world. Although they need older people to take care of them, they are aware of many things, such as who is holding them. As babies grow, they get better at letting others know what they need and understand more of what happens around them.

New babies need warm cuddles, milk and sleep. They can't talk, so they cry in different ways to let you know they are hungry, tired or uncomfortable.

Very young babies learn how to raise their heads. They are soon strong enough to move around and explore.

Babies are always looking, learning and touching things. Once they learn to do something, they may do it over and over again.

As their brains and muscles develop, babies begin to walk. At first, they may hold on to something or someone bigger. But between the ages of one and two, toddlers usually start to walk alone.

Babies do not need teeth, but they have a whole set waiting inside their gums. These teeth start to come through when they are about six months old.

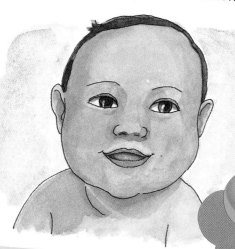

When they are first born, the only sound babies can make is to cry. They soon start to laugh and make other noises that sound more like words after a year or so.

Tiny babies can only suck milk from a bottle or from their mother, but they quickly learn to eat cereal and then to chew their food.

Babies and toddlers need people to take care of them. They soon learn to recognize their carers.

Blood

Blood is a thick, red liquid that carries **oxygen** and food to every part of your body. It also collects **waste** and takes it to the places that can get rid of it. Special **cells** in your blood fight **germs** and help to repair your body when you get hurt. Your blood is pumped through your body by your heart. Blood flows into your heart before each beat, then your heart squeezes it out to continue its journey.

Red or blue?

Red blood cells carry oxygen collected from your lungs to the parts of your body that need it. When they have delivered the oxygen, the cells turn blue. Outside the body, your blood always looks red, because the cells turn red as soon as they touch the oxygen in the air.

arteries
Your arteries are vessels which carry blood away from your heart to the rest of your body.

The veins carry blood back to your heart. Sometimes they show through your skin as bluish lines. You may be able to see them inside your elbow or wrist. Your arteries are deeper down in your body than your veins.

heart
Your heart is about the same size as your fist. It is made of strong muscle, which pushes almost five litres of blood through your blood vessels every minute.

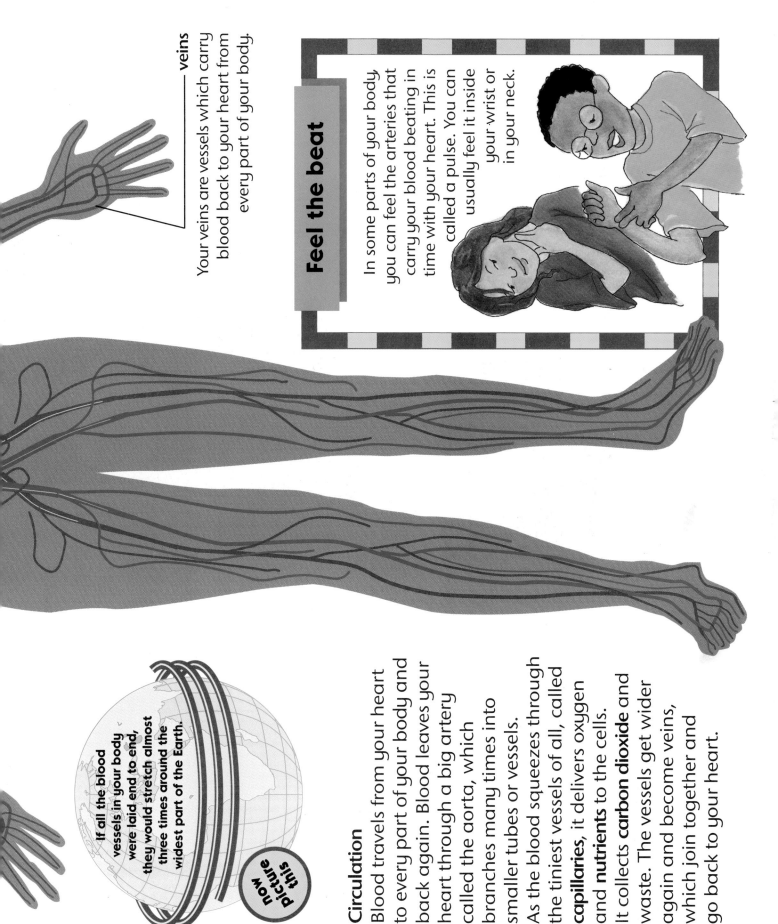

veins

Your veins are vessels which carry blood back to your heart from every part of your body.

Feel the beat

In some parts of your body, you can feel the arteries that carry your blood beating in time with your heart. This is called a pulse. You can usually feel it inside your wrist or in your neck.

If all the blood vessels in your body were laid end to end, they would stretch almost three times around the widest part of the Earth.

now picture this

Circulation

Blood travels from your heart to every part of your body and back again. Blood leaves your heart through a big artery called the aorta, which branches many times into smaller tubes or vessels. As the blood squeezes through the tiniest vessels of all, called **capillaries,** it delivers oxygen and **nutrients** to the cells. It collects **carbon dioxide** and waste. The vessels get wider again and become veins, which join together and go back to your heart.

Body

Your body is a living factory. It has billions of workers called **cells. There are many types of cells that work together to form the parts of your body, like your skin, heart, blood and bones. All the parts work together to keep the factory running smoothly. Your body needs food, water and oxygen to grow and breathe.**

brain

Your brain is your body's control centre. It sends and receives signals along **nerves.** The nerves connect your brain with every part of your body. Information about the world around you travels along your nerves. It helps you think and act.

heart

Your heart pumps your blood. Each time your heart beats, it squeezes blood down tubes, or vessels, that carry it to every part of your body. Your blood picks up and delivers oxygen, food and **waste** to the many different cells in your body.

lungs

When you breathe, you suck air into your lungs, then blow it out again. Oxygen from the air is collected from your lungs by your blood.

stomach

Your stomach and intestines are part of your **digestive system.**

intestines

16

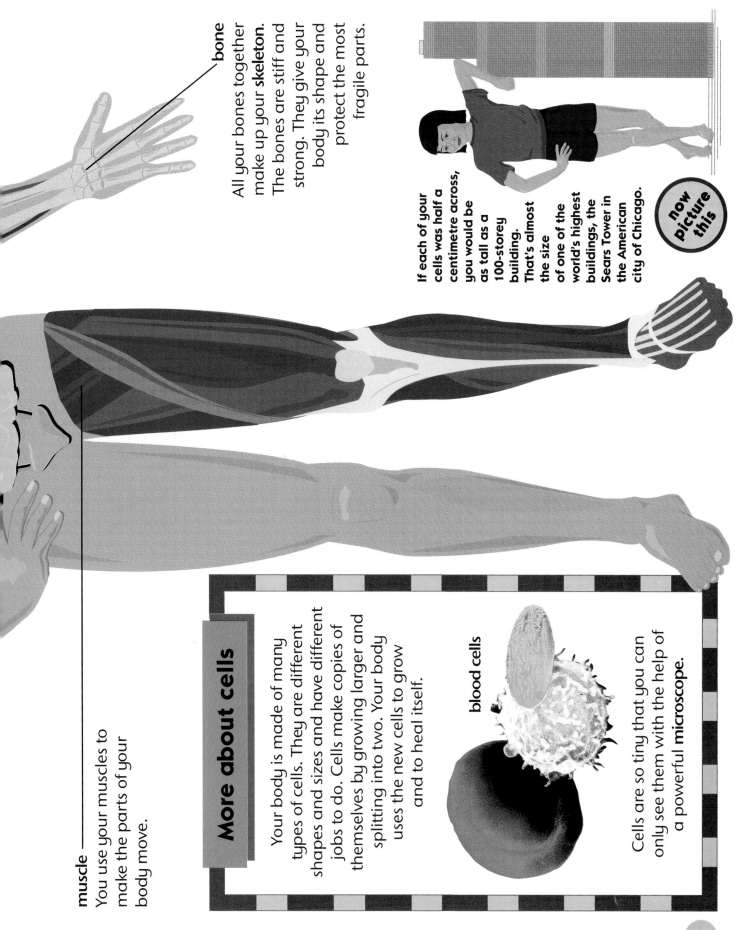

bone

All your bones together make up your **skeleton**. The bones are stiff and strong. They give your body its shape and protect the most fragile parts.

muscle

You use your muscles to make the parts of your body move.

If each of your cells was half a centimetre across, you would be as tall as a 100-storey building. That's almost the size of one of the world's highest buildings, the Sears Tower in the American city of Chicago.

now picture this

More about cells

Your body is made of many types of cells. They are different shapes and sizes and have different jobs to do. Cells make copies of themselves by growing larger and splitting into two. Your body uses the new cells to grow and to heal itself.

blood cells

Cells are so tiny that you can only see them with the help of a powerful **microscope**.

17

Bone

Bones fit together to form the **skeleton** inside your body. Your skeleton has 206 different bones which are made from a stony **substance** called **calcium.** They feel hard and rough, but they are alive, just like the softer parts of your body. Your bones help to give your body its shape and strength. They also **protect** the more fragile parts, such as your brain and lungs.

skull
Your skull is a bony case that protects your brain.

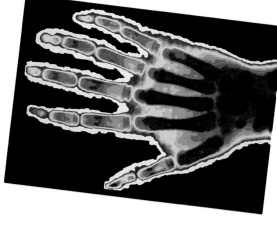

▲ X-rays are photographs that let you see bones. They can be coloured to give more information about the body.

spine
The spine or backbone protects the **nerves** in your spinal cord, and helps you to stand upright.

ribs
The ribs make a cage to protect your heart and lungs.

pelvis
The pelvis is the name given to your hipbones.

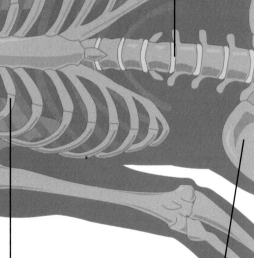

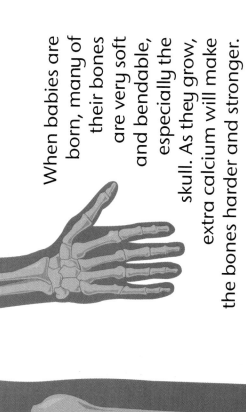

When babies are born, many of their bones are very soft and bendable, especially the skull. As they grow, extra calcium will make the bones harder and stronger.

Did you know?

Your funny bone is not really a bone. It is a nerve that runs through your elbow. When something touches the place where the nerve is, you get a funny feeling.

The smallest bones in your body are inside your ear. They are about the size of a grain of rice! Each ear has three of these bones that vibrate or shiver when sounds travel into your ears.

Broken bones

Bones make sure your body bends only in the right places. Your leg bends at the knee and ankle joints. If an accident forces your leg to bend in any other place, one or more of your leg bones might break. Bones are made up of tiny **cells** just like the other parts of your body. When they break, the cells grow to join the broken ends together again. A hard bandage called a cast is put around broken bones to protect them and hold them still, so that they can heal.

Marrow

The larger bones in your body are hard and solid on the outside but inside them is a much softer **substance** called marrow. The marrow in some of your bones makes new red blood cells.

Brain

▼ Different parts of your brain do different kinds of work. Some look after particular parts of your body.

Did you know?

A six year old has the same size brain as an adult! When you were born your brain weighed less than half a kilogram. By the time you are six, it will already have reached its full weight of about one and a half kilograms.

There is no blood inside your brain itself, although there are blood vessels around the outside of your brain.

This part helps you to talk.

This part helps you to think.

This part helps you to hear.

Your brain is a soft greyish-pink ball about the size of a grapefruit, **protected** by your bony skull. It works as your body's control box, receiving signals from your **senses** about what is going on around you and sending out messages to tell your body what to do. You use your brain to think, learn, remember, see, hear, touch and feel. Your brain also does work that you do not have to think about, such as breathing and making your heart beat.

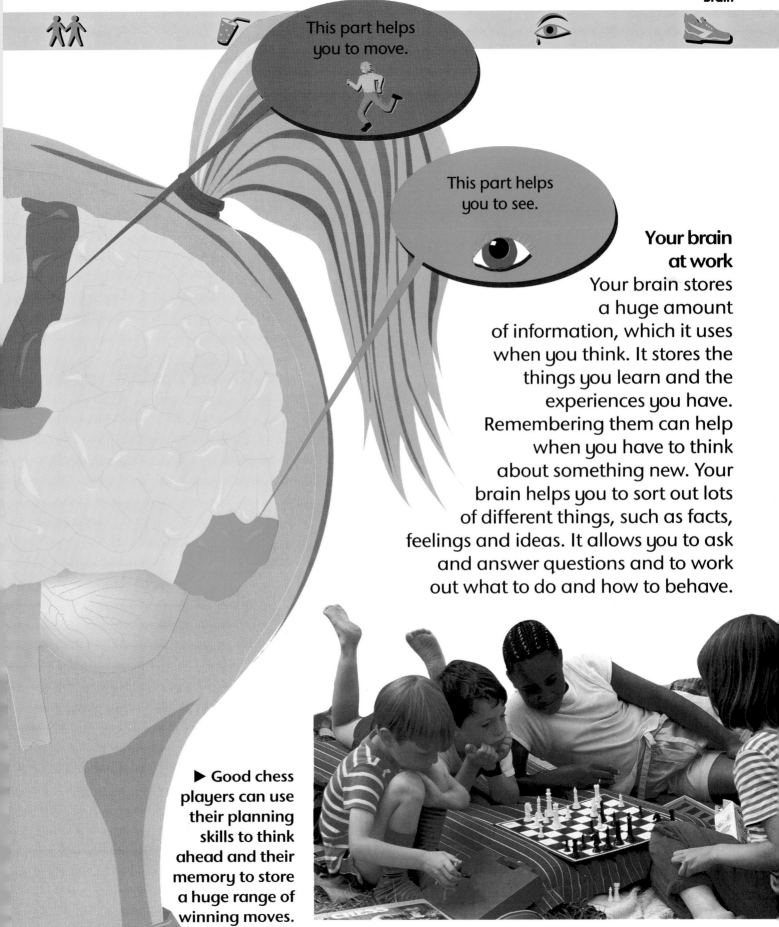

This part helps you to move.

This part helps you to see.

Your brain at work

Your brain stores a huge amount of information, which it uses when you think. It stores the things you learn and the experiences you have. Remembering them can help when you have to think about something new. Your brain helps you to sort out lots of different things, such as facts, feelings and ideas. It allows you to ask and answer questions and to work out what to do and how to behave.

▶ Good chess players can use their planning skills to think ahead and their memory to store a huge range of winning moves.

Young children

Like babies, young children are very curious. Unlike babies, they can ask questions. They are able to explore the world around them. They can run, jump and ride tricycles. They play with other people in their families, and they make other friends.

Young children love to draw, paint, sing songs and recite rhymes. Most are ready to go to nursery school and play with other kids.

Small children know they are no longer babies. They may even have their own baby brother or sister.

Sharing toys is very hard, but young children can learn to do it. It helps them to begin to understand the feelings of others.

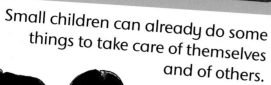
Small children can already do some things to take care of themselves and of others.

Children learn to use words to ask for things they want. They also begin to learn that they cannot always have everything they ask for.

Young children begin to discover more and more ways of learning about people, places and things.

23

Breathing

When you breathe, you suck air into your body through your nose and mouth, and blow it out again. The air goes down a tube in your throat and into your lungs, which are two stretchy, spongy bags in your chest. Air contains a **gas** called **oxygen**, which you need to stay alive. As you breathe, your blood collects the oxygen and takes it to every part of your body.

▲ When you blow bubbles, the air you breathe out is trapped inside.

Take a deep breath

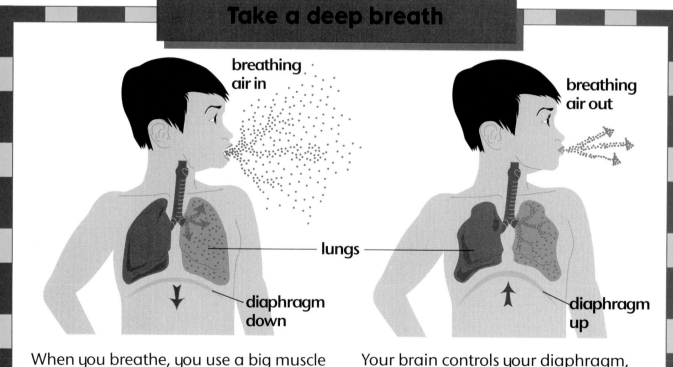

breathing air in

breathing air out

lungs

diaphragm down

diaphragm up

When you breathe, you use a big muscle just underneath your lungs. It is called your diaphragm (say "die-a-fram"). It pulls downwards to suck the air in and moves upwards to push out used air.

Your brain controls your diaphragm, telling it how often and how deeply to breathe. You can hold your breath for a short time but soon you will feel that you must breathe.

Your body needs the oxygen that you breathe to get **energy**. When you move fast or work hard, you use more energy. You have to breathe more quickly and take deeper breaths. When your **cells** take energy from food, they make a **waste** called **carbon dioxide**. Your blood takes this waste back to your lungs. You get rid of it when you breathe out.

▼ There is no oxygen to breathe on the Moon, so astronauts take their own supply of air with them.

Did you know?

Yawning is good for you! When you sit still, you take small breaths that only fill part of your lungs. A yawn stretches your lungs and keeps them fit.

No one knows why seeing someone else yawn makes you yawn too. Some scientists believe it happens because yawning is important, and your body needs to be reminded to do it.

Coughs and sneezes

Illnesses like colds or the flu can make your nose run. A liquid forms in your breathing tubes. This can block the tubes. A piece of food can sometimes block them, too. When this happens, you cough or sneeze, sending a blast of air along your breathing tubes to push away the block.

The air you breathe out when you sneeze can travel at up to 160 kilometres per hour, as fast as a powerful hurricane!

now picture this

Clothes

Clothes are a covering for your body. The right kind of clothing makes you feel comfortable, wherever you are. It keeps you warm in cold weather, dry in the rain, and **protects** your skin from being burned by the Sun. Clothes are made in many different styles. It is fun to choose the way you want to look by deciding what clothes to wear. Ideas about style and fashion are always changing. They vary from one country to another.

▲ Clothes made from fur or fluffy fibres hold warm air close to your body to protect against the cold.

Where clothes come from

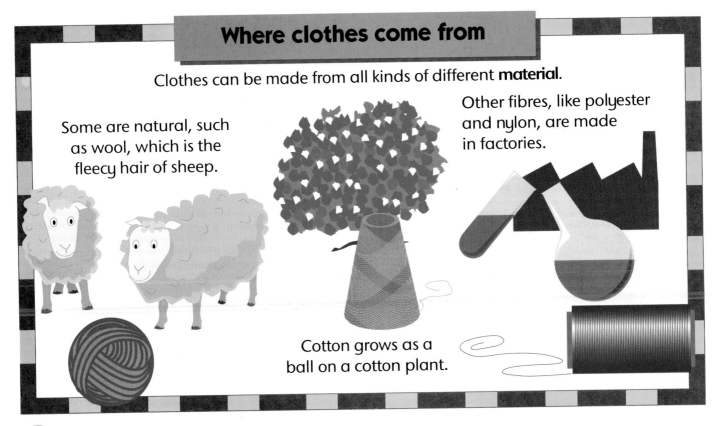

Clothes can be made from all kinds of different **material**.

Some are natural, such as wool, which is the fleecy hair of sheep.

Other fibres, like polyester and nylon, are made in factories.

Cotton grows as a ball on a cotton plant.

▲ Cotton clothes are good to wear on hot days. They let in fresh air and soak up sweat to keep your skin cool.

▼ Some factory-made fibres are waterproof. They have a special coating which water cannot pass through.

Special clothes give extra protection when it is needed. Divers wear rubber wet suits to keep out the cold. Hard hats or helmets protect workers against head injuries. Astronauts wear special clothes to control the air around their bodies.

▶ Clothes made from light, **flexible** materials allow people to move easily when they play sports.

▲ Special clothes stop this bee keeper from being stung.

Drinking

▼ When you get very hot, water leaves your body as sweat. You need to replace this water by drinking.

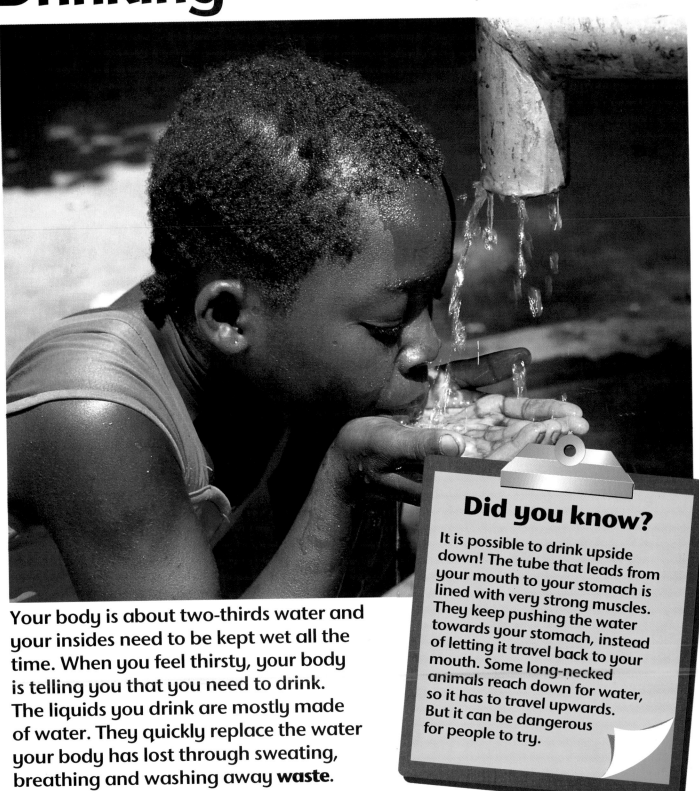

Your body is about two-thirds water and your insides need to be kept wet all the time. When you feel thirsty, your body is telling you that you need to drink. The liquids you drink are mostly made of water. They quickly replace the water your body has lost through sweating, breathing and washing away **waste**.

Did you know?

It is possible to drink upside down! The tube that leads from your mouth to your stomach is lined with very strong muscles. They keep pushing the water towards your stomach, instead of letting it travel back to your mouth. Some long-necked animals reach down for water, so it has to travel upwards. But it can be dangerous for people to try.

▲ All living things need water to survive. Animals and many people may have to travel long distances to find water to drink.

Washed away

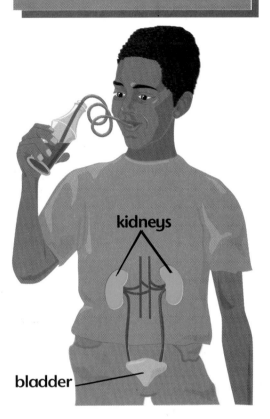

kidneys

bladder

Your kidneys take waste from your blood and remove the extra water that your body does not need. They make urine and pass it into your bladder where it collects. You get rid of urine when you go to the toilet.

Keeping cool

Your skin and lungs use water to keep your body cool, so on hot days you need to drink more and go to the toilet less. When you are too hot, you sweat and lose water through your skin. There is also a little water in the air your lungs breathe out. You can see this if you breathe onto a mirror or a pane of glass. The water turns from a **gas** back into tiny droplets that sit on the glass and make it look cloudy.

now picture this

In the hot African desert, there is a tree that stores up to half a litre of water in each of its stalks. It is called the traveller's tree and provides thirsty travellers with water to drink.

Feeling thirsty

When your body needs water, your mouth feels dry and may have a salty taste. Having a drink makes you feel better right away. Water travels through the skin of your mouth and stomach very quickly.

Eating

▼ Food gives you **energy**. It helps to keep you warm when the weather is cold.

When you eat, you chew and swallow food which you need to keep you alive. Your body lets you know that it needs food by making you feel hungry. Food is made of many different **substances**. You need some of these substances, such as **protein, carbohydrates** (say "car-bo-hi-drates") and fats to grow and stay healthy. When you have eaten, your body collects the substances it needs, leaving the leftovers to travel on through your **digestive system.**

fats,
oils, sweets

milk,
yoghurt, cheese

meat,
poultry, fish,
dry beans,
eggs, nuts

vegetables

fruits

bread, cereal,
grains, pasta

▲ Your body takes substances called **nutrients** from food. Most foods contain a mixture of nutrients. To stay healthy, it's best to eat lots of the foods at the bottom of this triangle, and just a little of the foods at the top.

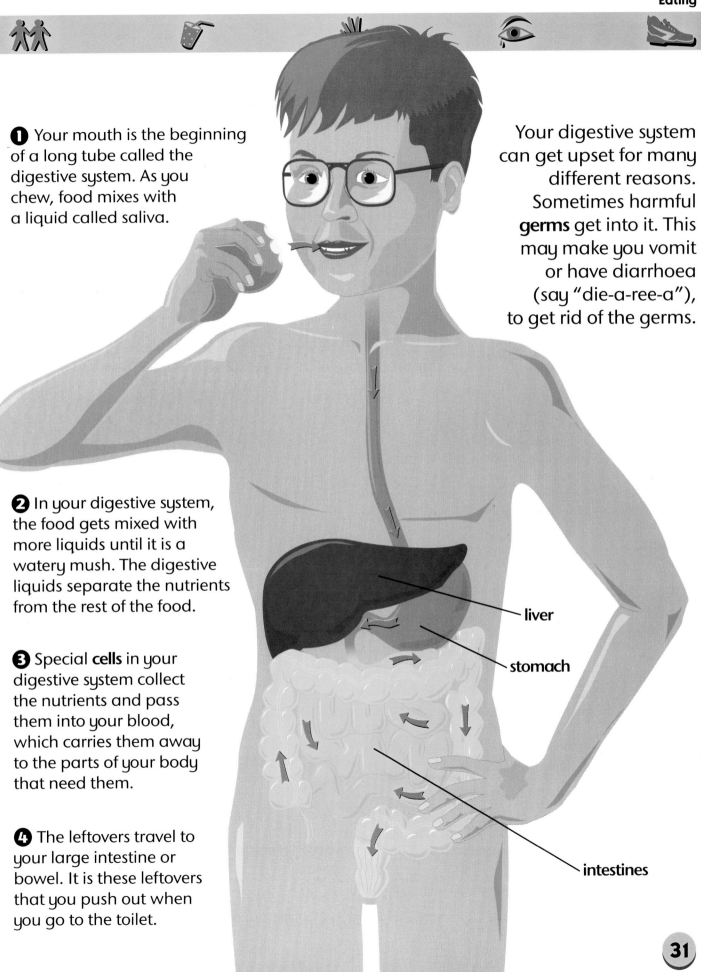

1 Your mouth is the beginning of a long tube called the digestive system. As you chew, food mixes with a liquid called saliva.

Your digestive system can get upset for many different reasons. Sometimes harmful **germs** get into it. This may make you vomit or have diarrhoea (say "die-a-ree-a"), to get rid of the germs.

2 In your digestive system, the food gets mixed with more liquids until it is a watery mush. The digestive liquids separate the nutrients from the rest of the food.

3 Special **cells** in your digestive system collect the nutrients and pass them into your blood, which carries them away to the parts of your body that need them.

4 The leftovers travel to your large intestine or bowel. It is these leftovers that you push out when you go to the toilet.

liver

stomach

intestines

31

Family

The people you live with are your family. Families come in all varieties. The adults and older children in a family look after and teach the younger ones. Sometimes they care for sick or elderly family members, too.

The people in a family are usually related to each other. Some children live in a large family with their mother, father, brothers, sisters, and even grandparents, uncles, and aunts. Other families are small, with just one parent and one or two children.

Anna's grandparents

Anna's grandparents

▶ A family tree shows how people in a family are related to each other.

Anna's parents

Anna's uncle

Anna's sister

Anna

Anna's brother

Anna's cousin

Some families also include special friends. Even pets can be part of a family. Families do all kinds of things with one another.

They eat, play, talk and do chores together. Even though families may not always get along, they are loyal to one another and stick by each other. Children usually stay with their family until they are grown up.

▶ You do not always have to be related to be part of a family.

Running in the family

Your body works and grows using instructions called **genes** that are inside all your body's **cells.** Your genes were passed on to you by your **biological** parents, half from your mother and half from your father. You may look like your relatives because your cells contain many of the same gene instructions.

Identical twins share exactly the same genes. **Fraternal** twins do not share identical qualities. They are more like sisters and brothers who happen to be born at the same time.

▲ Pairs of identical twins look exactly alike because they have the same genes.

Schoolchildren

School is a place for learning about yourself, other people and things. When you start to go to school, you become part of a group that is much bigger than your family. You meet people who may be like your family members or may be different. School has its own rules to help everyone get along.

Schoolchildren love to make things. They can even make complicated things because they have become more coordinated.

Most children look forward to starting school. This may be the year they learn to read. They recognize more and more what is real and what is imaginary.

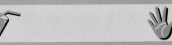

Playtime is important. Exercise makes you stronger. Children in school can play group games now.

As they get older, schoolchildren can learn to do more and more for themselves and to help others.

By the time you go to school, your brain has grown to its full size. You will learn more as you get older, but your brain won't become any bigger, just more full.

See also Friend; HOW THINGS WORK Roller coaster

Feelings

You have feelings about everything that happens to you. You may feel happy or sad, excited or bored, relaxed or worried, calm or angry. You show your feelings in the way you behave. Strong feelings can make you laugh or cry.

▼ Some people like to watch scary films or take roller coaster rides. They enjoy feeling scared.

▲ Some people feel best doing things their own way, while others prefer to follow the crowd.

Everyone has feelings, but the same things can make different people feel totally different. For example, some people love to have time alone. Others feel lonely if they are on their own for even a short time. Some people like spiders and others feel afraid of them.

▶ A good way to stop being frightened of spiders is to learn more about them.

▲ Clowns help us to show our feelings when they make us laugh.

What's so funny?

Laughter is a happy sound and it feels good. It shows others that you like them and are having fun being with them. Laughter often begins with a smile that turns into giggles. Sometimes you just burst out laughing. It can be difficult to stop, and laughing hard can even make you cry.

Feeling sad

You usually cry when you feel very sad or extremely frightened or even very happy. Sometimes you just cannot stop yourself from crying. Tears spill out of your eyes and run down your face. Crying lets other people know how you really feel. A good cry can sometimes make you feel better if you're unhappy.

What are tears?

Tears are a washing liquid to keep your eyes clean. They are squeezed out by **glands** behind your eyelids and they drain away at the inside corners of your eyes. They run down the inside of your nose, which is why it runs when you cry.

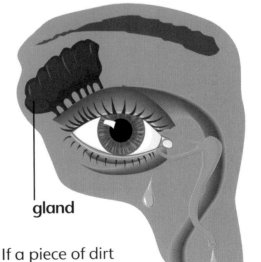

gland

If a piece of dirt gets into your eye, tears help to wash it out. Peeling onions can have the same effect because air carries a **chemical** from the onion into your eye.

Friend

A friend is someone you know, like and trust. You may have one best friend or you may be friendly with several people. Friends like to do things together and help each other out. Although you do not always agree with a friend, you want what is best for that person. You may argue, but you do not stop caring. And your friend feels exactly the same way about you.

Friends usually have a lot in common. This helps them to understand each other and have fun together. Friends can be quite different from each other, too. Elderly people can be friends with younger people.

▲ People often become friends because they enjoy doing the same things.

It's a special feeling to have a good friend and to be a good friend. You can be friends with someone in your neighbourhood or someone at school. Friends make everything much more fun.

You may find that after talking or playing with someone a few times you really enjoy being with that person. Friends are an important part of the world around you.

Being a friend

Being a friend means caring for another person and trying to do things that will please that person. Sharing and understanding, being considerate and thoughtful, all play an important part in making a friendship.

Hair

Hair grows from tiny tubes in your skin called follicles. Hair is thickest on top of your head and does not grow at all in some places, such as the soles of your feet. Hair helps to **protect** you from the sun and cold. It keeps dust and dirt out of your eyes, ears and nose. Your hair lets you feel things before they touch your skin. It also plays a big part in the way you look.

Curly or straight?

The shape of hairs and their follicles makes hair either straight, wavy or curly. If you sliced through a straight hair, it would look round, while a wavy hair would look oval and a curly hair would look rectangular.

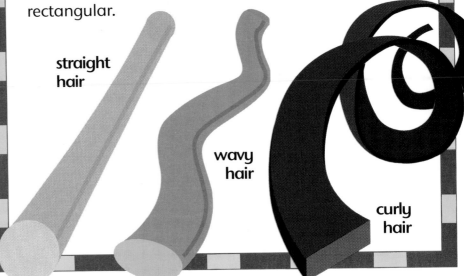

straight hair

wavy hair

curly hair

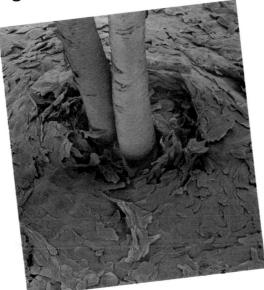

▲ These hairs and their follicles are shown many times bigger than they really are.

It's hair-raising!

Every one of your hairs has its own **nerve** right underneath your skin. If the hair moves, the nerve sends a signal to your brain to let you know there is a breeze, even if it is very faint. Each hair also has its own tiny muscle. If something frightens you, the muscle pulls on the hair and it stands up. This gives you goose pimples.

Hair changes as people get older. Adults have more hair all over their bodies than children, and it grows coarser. Men have bristly hair growing on their faces. As people get older, they often stop making the **cells** that give their hair its colour, so it turns white.

▲ This woman's ceremonial hairstyle takes almost three hours to do. She sleeps with her neck on a wooden pillow to keep the hairstyle in place for a week.

Healing

Your body is an amazing machine that can mend itself. It can clear away dirt and **germs** and grow new skin, muscles or bone to repair an injury. Of course, a little sympathy helps, too.

Bumps and bruises

The tubes that carry your blood are often damaged when you hurt yourself. If you cut your skin, blood may leak out. If you just get a bump, you may see the blood as a bruise under your skin.

▼ Covering a wound helps to **protect** it while it heals.

Heal up!

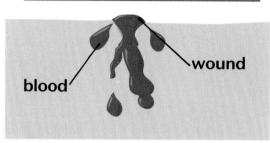

Bleeding stops when the blood coming out of a wound becomes thicker and plugs up the leak.

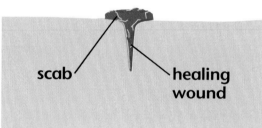

The blood seals the wound with a hard crust called a scab.

The way your body looks and feels when you hurt yourself lets you know something is wrong. Extra blood goes to the damaged place, so it may look red and swollen. Special **cells** in your blood start to repair the damage. They clear away any dirt or germs that are around it.

▶ An ice pack helps to soothe bruises.

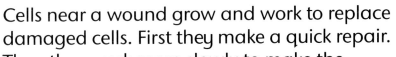

Cells near a wound grow and work to replace damaged cells. First they make a quick repair. Then they work more slowly to make the injured place look as good as new. They cannot always make it look exactly as it did before it was hurt. A bad wound may leave a scar.

▶ This girl's broken arm has been wrapped in a hard **substance** called plaster. The plaster protects the arm and keeps the bones from moving so that they can heal properly.

When a part of your body hurts, the feeling can stop you from doing too much damage to yourself. If you touch something hot, you get an urgent warning. It makes you take your hand away very quickly. This helps to stop you from burning yourself badly. Afterwards, the burned skin may keep feeling sore until it has healed. This makes you take extra care of the damaged place while it is healing.

❶ A warning goes from your finger to your brain.

❷ Your brain tells the muscles in your arm to move your finger away from the heat.

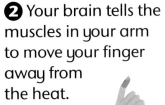

Preteens

Preteens usually have a period when they seem to grow taller very quickly. This often happens to girls about a year earlier than it does to boys. As preteens develop more adult bodies, they start to think about grown-up things and what it will be like to be an adult. Families are still important, of course, but preteens begin spending more time outside the family.

Preteens usually pay a lot more attention to how they look than they did as children.

Preteens often become expert at something and learn to do it better than anyone else in the family. They may like particular sports, or dance, sing or act very well.

Preteens often have crushes on film stars, musicians and famous athletes.

Going away on school trips or with friends helps preteens find out how it feels to be away from their family. They realize they have lots in common with other children and adults.

For preteens, the closest friendships are usually with people of their own sex, girls with girls, boys with boys. Boys may feel shy with girls and girls with boys.

Hearing

Hearing is the **sense** that lets you know about sounds. Your ears and brain work together to tell you what sounds are and where they come from. This helps you to understand what is happening around you and to listen and talk to other people. Hearing sounds can sometimes help you work out what to expect. You can also listen to sounds such as music just for fun.

You can remember certain sounds well, especially voices. Your brain began learning to understand voices the moment you first heard someone talk. You also learn to tell who is speaking from the sound of their voice. A baby quickly recognizes its mother's voice.

▶ You can hear the sound of a drum from far away. People once used drums to send messages over long distances.

❶ When something makes a noise, it shivers or vibrates. You can feel the vibrations if you touch the loudspeakers when the stereo is playing. The air around them moves too. The outer parts of your ears work as sound collectors. They pick up the shivers or vibrations from the air.

ear

❷ The vibrations travel down a tunnel inside your ear. They reach your eardrum. It is a tiny piece of skin stretched tightly across the end of the tunnel.

Hearing tells you how loud or soft a sound is and whether it is a high squeak or a low rumble. Children can often hear sounds that adults cannot hear. As people get older, it is harder for them to hear quiet or high sounds. Some people who cannot hear well use a hearing aid to make sounds louder. Those who cannot hear at all can learn to talk using signs, or by watching someone's lips move as they speak. This is called lipreading.

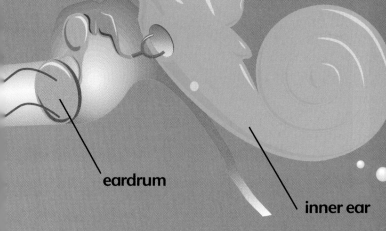

eardrum

inner ear

❸ When your eardrum moves, each tiny shiver is picked up by **nerves** in your inner ear. They send messages to your brain about the sounds you hear.

❹ Millions of these sound signals reach your brain every second. It quickly sorts them out so that you know what you are listening to.

Joint

Your joints are where your bones meet. You have joints everywhere that your body needs to bend. The bones in a joint are held together by strong, stretchy bands, or ligaments, which make the joint **flexible**.

Your shoulders, elbows, hips and knees are all joints. There are several different types of joints that let parts such as your arms, legs and backbone move in various ways.

Types of joint

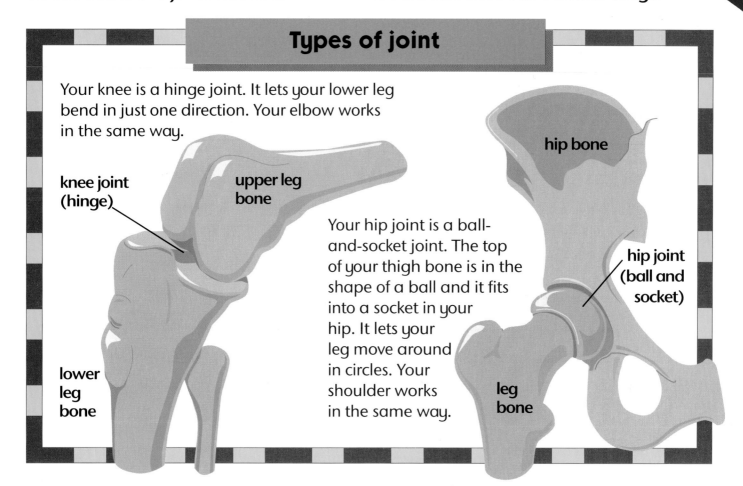

Your knee is a hinge joint. It lets your lower leg bend in just one direction. Your elbow works in the same way.

knee joint (hinge)

upper leg bone

lower leg bone

Your hip joint is a ball-and-socket joint. The top of your thigh bone is in the shape of a ball and it fits into a socket in your hip. It lets your leg move around in circles. Your shoulder works in the same way.

hip bone

hip joint (ball and socket)

leg bone

When you bend a joint, the ends of each bone slide against one another. To make sure they slide smoothly, the bones have a special covering. There is also a layer of liquid between them to stop them from creaking.

Joints do sometimes make clicking and popping noises. This is because tiny air bubbles get stirred up in the joint liquid. When you move in certain ways, you squeeze these bubbles and they pop.

▼ Many dancers move very easily because their joints are loose and supple.

Did you know?

You will probably flex the joints in your fingers about twenty five million times during your life.

Double-jointed people actually have the same number of joints as others. They can bend and twist some parts of their body further because their ligaments are very loose, making them more supple.

Out of joint
Joints can become dislocated. This means that the bones are not meeting properly. Usually, a doctor has to pull or push the bones back into place before they stop hurting and begin to heal.

Bend and stretch
Your ligaments are meant to stretch. But if you make them stretch too far by accident, you can damage a joint. If you tear a ligament, you must rest it for a while to give it a chance to heal. Stretching a torn ligament hurts, to help you remember to rest it.

Learning

Learning is finding out about things. When you learn something new, it can help you understand the world around you. You can also learn to do things better, such as play a sport or a musical instrument. You are learning all the time. Sometimes you learn just by remembering a sound, a feeling or a taste. At other times, learning can be hard work, but it feels good to know you are getting wiser and becoming more skillful.

► People learn different skills at their own rate. An acrobat may take several years to learn to juggle and ride a unicycle.

You can learn to do some things very quickly, with little help or practice, such as playing simple games. A more difficult skill, reading or writing for instance, can take much longer to learn and you may need help. With learning most new things, you will have to practise to get really good at them.

◄ Babies usually learn to walk at about a year old, but at first they need help to balance and stay on their feet.

Learning takes place all the time. You began to learn from the moment you were born. When you were a toddler, you watched and listened to other people and patiently practised walking and talking. You will learn all kinds of things throughout your life. The more you learn the more interesting life becomes.

Sometimes you can only remember things for a few moments. Other things will stay in your memory for many years. Scientists are still trying to understand how memories are stored in the brain. **Nerve cells** pass on messages from your brain all the time. They make millions of new connections every second. Using these connections again and again may be how your brain learns and remembers.

▲ Children study many subjects at school to help them learn the skills they will need as they grow up.

▲ Learning to swim takes practice and help.

Moving

Moving gets you where you want to go. It lets you change the position of your whole body or any part of it. It also means you can pick things up and take them along with you. When you want to make your body move, you send messages from your brain to your muscles. Some parts of you, such as your heart, keep moving all the time without these messages. Your body's **cells** are always moving, too.

Balance

Just as your muscles make you move, they also have to stop you falling over by keeping you balanced. You have two balance **detectors** inside your head, near your ears. Each has three small tubes filled with liquid.

When you move around, this liquid moves, too. Cells in the lining of the tubes send messages to your brain about how the liquid is moving. This helps your brain control your muscles that keep you standing up.

When you want to move, **nerves** carry messages to the right muscles telling them to work. They send messages back to tell your brain exactly how far they have moved. This lets your brain control each movement perfectly.

When your muscles need to work very quickly, you do not have to tell them to move. When something suddenly comes towards your eyes, they blink. You cannot stop them. This is called a reflex action.

▼ Gymnasts learn to control their movements and stay balanced, even turning a cartwheel on a narrow beam.

Teenagers

During the teenage years, a person's body goes through the final changes towards becoming an adult. Teenagers are no longer children. They could even have children of their own, but most prefer to spend this stage of their lives learning more about the world.

Teenagers are old enough to go out without their parents. For the first time, they can do things by themselves, without any adults around.

Being a teenager can feel like having a new body.

Looking good is important to most teenagers. They need to keep fit if they want to look their best.

Lots of exciting things are happening in teenagers' lives outside school. But they still need to study, because their education will make a big difference to their future lives.

Most teenagers start going out on dates and develop close friendships with other people their age. They may seem to have little time for their families.

Having a job for the first time can be fun, even if it is hard work. It feels good having money you have earned yourself.

Muscle

Muscles make your body move. When you want to move a part of your body, your brain works out which muscles are needed. Then it sends messages to these muscles, telling them to move your bones. Thousands of muscles are attached to the bones of your **skeleton.**

You also have different kinds of muscles which do other important jobs. Your heart is a muscle which pumps your blood around your body. Muscles in your stomach mix your food and push it on through your **digestive system.** A muscle under your lungs makes you breathe.

When muscles work, they make themselves shorter to pull a part of your body and make it move.

When you want to bend your elbow, a muscle on the upper part of your arm gets shorter, pulling your lower arm upwards. This muscle is called the biceps (say "by-seps").

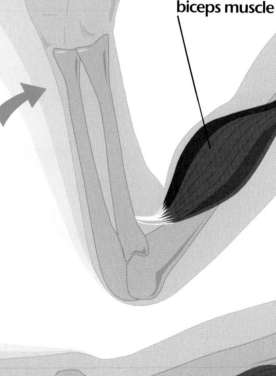

biceps muscle

When you want to straighten your elbow, the triceps (say "try-seps") muscle on the other side of your upper arm takes over and pulls it straight.

triceps muscle

▼ Exercise helps to build up strong muscles. An athlete needs well-developed muscles to be fit and fast.

Each of your movement muscles is linked to your brain by **nerves** that carry messages back and forth. Your brain tells the muscle to pull and it sends a message back to let your brain know how much it has pulled. This way, your brain controls all your muscle movements.

now picture this

If you had the same muscle power as an ant, you would be strong enough to lift a car!

Getting fit
If you make your muscles work hard, they grow and change to become more efficient. Muscles get stronger by growing bigger so that they can pull harder. They grow extra blood vessels to carry more blood into the muscle. The blood brings more **oxygen** so the muscles can work longer without getting tired.

People with big muscles are strong, but not always fitter than people with smaller muscles. Bodybuilders lift weights regularly to make their muscles bigger. Dancers are often much fitter, although their muscles may be less bulky. They can dance for many hours without getting tired.

Shiver and shake

Working hard makes you sweat even on a cold day, because muscles warm up when they work. If you need to warm yourself up, your brain tells your muscles to shiver.

Playing

Playing is fun and it also helps you learn about the world around you. You can play with another person, with many people, or by yourself. There are games and sports to play, or you can make-believe. Playing is often a break from working and a time to do things that you enjoy doing. Everyone needs to spend time playing. Even the grown-ups around you need to play. Having fun helps you to relax, which feels good too.

▲ **Playing together**
is a good way to make new friends.

Young babies find out about the world around them as they play. They use their ears, eyes and hands to learn about their new world. As they grow older, the way they play changes. You can play more exciting games now than you could when you were younger.

◄ People of different ages enjoy different kinds of play, but they can play together, too. Playing with other people helps you to get to know them.

Playing is best when everyone has a chance to have fun. It is important to share and let everyone join in when you play so that all your playmates will have a good time.

▶ **You can pretend to be anyone you like when you disguise yourself with face paints.**

You can play in different ways. Sometimes playing is very organized, such as a sport or board game. It's also fun just to mess about. Sometimes you need things to play with such as toys, a computer or dressing-up clothes. At other times, you can just use your imagination to have fun.

▲ You need an open space, such as a park or a field, and a good breeze to fly a kite.

Safety

To enjoy the world around you, you need to know about safety. You and your family should decide on certain rules that you should follow. As you grow up, you will know more and more about how to behave in a safe manner, no matter what you are doing.

▲ Sometimes, knowing you are safe from danger can be exciting and fun.

There are certain safety rules you must always follow when you are near a road or water, or out in a crowd. Remember what grown-ups teach you about safety and use your common sense. If you are on your own at home, do not tell someone over the phone that you are alone and do not answer the door.

◀ Some sports can be dangerous. Climbers use ropes, harnesses and helmets to help them stay safe.

▶ A life jacket keeps you afloat in the water. You should always wear one if you are on or near water.

Safety away from home

Never go anywhere with a stranger. Say "no" if you do not feel safe with someone. If anyone hurts you or makes you feel uncomfortable, even if it is someone you know, always tell your parents or a grown-up you trust.

If you get lost, try not to panic. Remember what you have been told by your family. It's a good idea to know your full name, your parents' names, and your telephone number and address. You and your family may also want to have a code word.

Walking safely
When you obey safety rules, other people know what to expect. It prevents accidents. When you walk on the pavement, try to stay away from the side of the road. When you cross a street, look in both directions first. Obey traffic lights and signs.

Seeing

Your **sense** of sight gives you a picture of what is happening around you. Your eyes pick up light as it shines from the Sun or from a light bulb. Light **rays** bounce off everything you look at. Your eyes send messages about the light to your brain. It turns them into a picture. You use your eyes all the time as you learn and grow and explore the world around you.

▲ If you wear goggles or a face mask, you can see as well underwater as you can on land.

❶ The clear part at the front of your eye is called the cornea. It lets in light from the world around you. It bends the light rays and sends them inside your eye.

Light rays go in through a small hole called the pupil. Your pupil is the black dot at the centre of your eye.

cornea

lens

pupil

▶ This diagram is a cross-section of an eye, shown from the side.

Why wear glasses?

Glasses or contact lenses bend the light a little more than usual before it goes into your eye. They help to **focus** the light. Without this help, short-sighted people can only see things clearly if they are close. Long-sighted people can only see things clearly if they are further away.

short-sighted

long-sighted

Our two eyes point in the same direction, which is forwards. Each eye sees a slightly different picture. The brain combines the two pictures into one. This is called binocular vision.

eyeball

retina

2 The light shines through the lens. The rays bend again. They focus a picture of what you are looking at on a screen at the back of your eye.

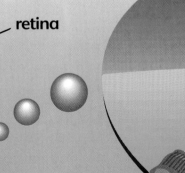

3 The screen is called the retina. It can sense the light and send messages about it to your brain. Pictures shine upside down on your retina. Your brain quickly turns them the right way up.

Sickness

▼ These **germs** cause measles. They are shown thousands of times bigger than they really are, and are colour-stained so you can see them better.

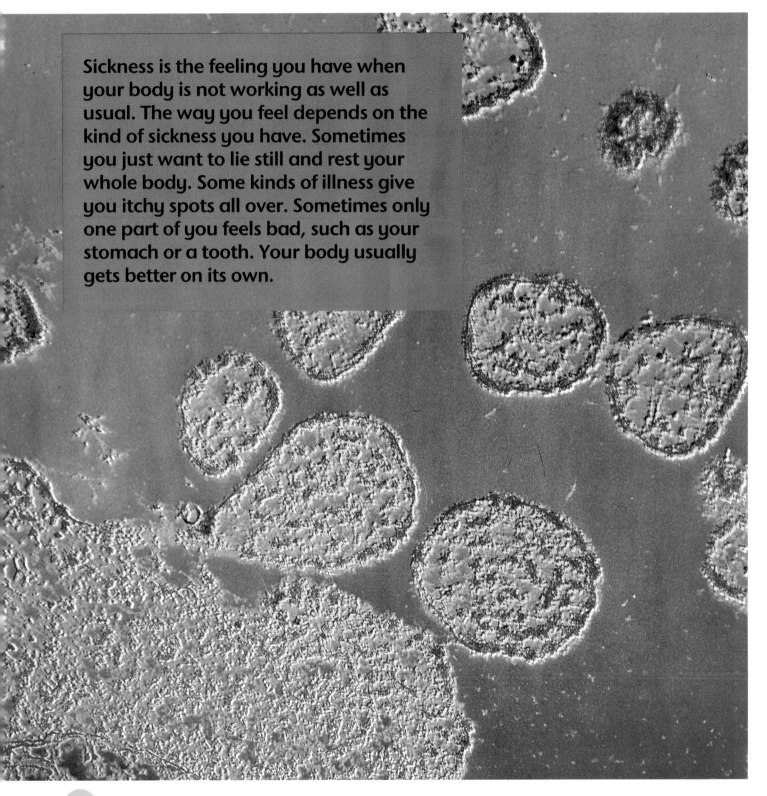

Sickness is the feeling you have when your body is not working as well as usual. The way you feel depends on the kind of sickness you have. Sometimes you just want to lie still and rest your whole body. Some kinds of illness give you itchy spots all over. Sometimes only one part of you feels bad, such as your stomach or a tooth. Your body usually gets better on its own.

What makes me sick?

Sickness is often caused by tiny living things called germs. There are many different kinds and most do you no harm, but a few cause illnesses such as colds, the flu and measles. Other germs make a part of your body hurt. When they live in your ear, you get an earache and when they live in your throat, it feels sore.

Your body gets rid of germs if they get into the wrong place by sending special **cells** to fight them. Although you wash and keep your skin clean, millions of germs live on the outside of your body all the time. Most of them are harmless, but some can cause warts or itchy athlete's foot.

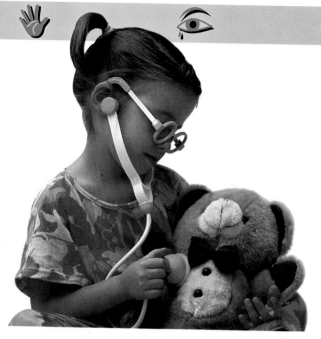

▲ When real doctors want to check on a patient's heartbeat or breathing, they use an instrument called a stethoscope.

▶ If you feel sick, you may have your **temperature** measured with a thermometer. This is a way of finding out if you have a high fever.

Clean up!

Your body has special ways of keeping itself clean and getting rid of germs and **waste chemicals**. You need to wash to keep germs out, too.

Taking a bath or shower, washing your hair, brushing your teeth and keeping your hands clean all help you to stay healthy.

Skin

Skin is the thin, stretchy, waterproof wrapper that covers your body. It is made up of layers, each with its own job. Your skin **protects** your insides from the outside world and lets you know what is happening in that world through your **sense** of touch. Skin also helps to stop your body from getting too hot or too cold.

▶ This diagram shows what happens under the surface of your skin.

Nerves carry messages to your brain about everything that touches your skin.

hair

skin

pore

old skin cells
new skin cells

nerve

sweat gland

sebaceous gland

capillaries

Sebaceous (say "se-bay-shus") **glands** make oil and squeeze it out to the surface of your skin to keep it soft and waterproof. The skin inside your ears makes extra oil, which turns into a sticky wax to keep dirt and **germs** out.

Water and salt from your blood are squeezed out of your skin by sweat glands, to help cool you down.

When you are hot, you may look red because the **capillaries** near the surface of your skin open wider to let more blood reach the cool air around you. This helps you cool down.

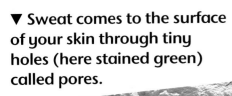

▼ Sweat comes to the surface of your skin through tiny holes (here stained green) called pores.

now picture this

People who live in very hot countries can lose as much as 11 litres of sweat in one day!

Special skin **cells** make coloured **substances** called pigments that help stop your skin being burned by the Sun. The cells squirt colour into the lower layer of your skin. People have different coloured skin because of these cells. When you are out in strong sunlight, your body produces more of the protective pigments, making your skin darker. But it is important to cover up or protect your skin with sunscreen whenever you are in the sun.

▶ The top layer of your skin is made up of dead cells. New layers are being made underneath all the time.

Did you know?

When you wash your skin, you actually wash it away. The old skin comes off in tiny flakes. About 200 grams of skin flakes off your body every year!

Pigs are mammals that do not have much hair on their bodies. Like fair-skinned people, they can suffer from sunburn.

▶ The skin that covers the palms of your hands and the soles of your feet has ridges, similar to the tread of a car tyre, to give you a good grip. These ridges create the patterns of your fingerprints.

Sleeping

When you sleep your eyes close and certain parts of your body rest. Your heart and lungs work more slowly when you sleep. Your muscles barely work at all. But your bones keep on growing, and your blood **cells** are very busy.

Some people walk.

Your body changes position while you sleep. Some people do funny things in their sleep.

Some people talk.

I'll feed the dinosaur!

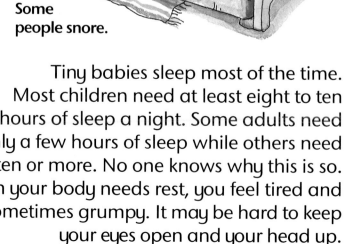

Some people snore.

Tiny babies sleep most of the time. Most children need at least eight to ten hours of sleep a night. Some adults need only a few hours of sleep while others need ten or more. No one knows why this is so. When your body needs rest, you feel tired and sometimes grumpy. It may be hard to keep your eyes open and your head up.

Dreaming

When you first go to sleep, your brain rests for a while. Then you start dreaming. When you dream, your brain works and thinks in almost the same way as it does when you are awake, but your body moves much less. Most people dream from three to five times during eight hours of sleep. Most dreams last from five to thirty minutes each. This pattern continues all night long.

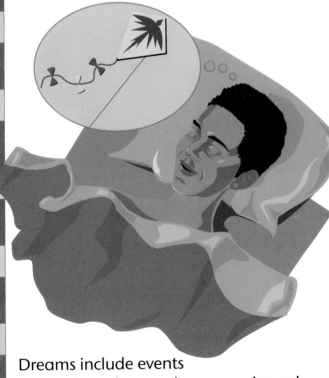

Dreams include events and feelings that you have experienced. Most dreams are related to things that happened the day of the dream.

Did you know?

You only remember the things you dream just before you wake up.

Dolphins sleep with one eye open.

If you went without sleep for two nights, you would find it hard to do a simple thing like saying your ABC.

▶ Animals need rest too. Bats usually sleep hanging upside down.

Smelling

Smells come from **chemicals** that float in the air. Your nose picks up smells when you breathe in. Your **sense** of smell can help you to find out about the world around you. Smells are invisible and can let you know about things you cannot see. Your sense of smell tells you that there are biscuits in the oven and warns you if they start to burn.

❶ Smelly things give off chemicals that travel through the air. As you breathe in, some of the chemicals get trapped for a while in the slimy **mucus** inside your nose.

❷ Your smell **detector cells** are in a small patch under the mucus. These cells send messages to your brain about the chemicals that are trapped in the mucus. Smell detectors can recognize about 3,000 different chemicals.

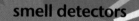

smell detectors

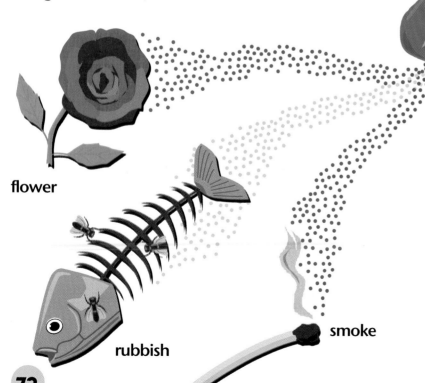

flower

rubbish

smoke

good smell

bad smell

warning smell

Sometimes you have a feeling about a smell before you recognize it. Your smell detectors send messages to the part of your brain that controls your feelings.

❸ Most smells are made up of a mixture of chemicals. You can learn to recognize many thousands more of these mixtures.

Did you know?

When you smell food cooking, you often feel hungry and your mouth waters.

Smelling can save lives, too. The smell of smoke is usually the first warning of a fire.

A dog's nose picks up smells about a million times better than yours can!

New smells can be very strong at first but they soon seem to go away. Your smell detectors get used to them after a while. If you have a cold and a stuffy nose, your sense of smell stops working. Food loses some of its taste because your smell and taste detectors work closely together.

Sports

Most sports exercise your brain as well as your body. To learn and improve, you need plenty of practice. As you become fitter and healthier, moving in the right way becomes easier. Your muscles grow stronger and your brain learns how to control them better.

◀ Crowds of people watch their favourite teams or athletes in a sports stadium.

Did you know?

Before the Olympic Games can begin, cross-country runners bring a lighted torch all the way to the stadium from Olympia in Greece, where the Olympics were first held. Ships and planes carry the torch over mountains and seas.

The highest board anyone has ever dived from was nearly as high as an 18-storey building.

Sports are a kind of play. Most sports give your body exercise and help you get fit and learn to use your muscles in different ways. Playing a sport can be hard work but it can also be fun. Sports are a good way to make new friends, whether you take part or just watch.

Some sports have winners and losers. These include team sports like football and games like tennis where one person plays against another. Sports like cross-country skiing and aerobics (say "air-o-bix") can be played alone or with others. No matter what you play, it feels good to do your best.

◀ People all over the world play sports, but certain sports, such as skiing, are more popular in some countries than others. People go skiing where there are mountains and cold, snowy weather.

Some sports have been played for thousands of years. Long ago, people needed to use a bow and arrow or a spear to hunt food and defend themselves. Archery and javelin contests helped people become more skillful and made practising more fun.

To enjoy a sport, it is important not to take risks. To **protect** your body and keep yourself and other players safe, you may need to wear special equipment.

▲ Helmets, face masks and pads help to protect American football players from injury.

75

Mature adults

As adults grow older, their lives may get busier and more complicated. Some grown-ups live both with their children and with their parents. At work, they often have a lot of responsibility. They may also contribute to their communities.

Many adults worry about getting wrinkles and grey hair, but these are only changes to the outside of their bodies. It's important for adults to stay fit, even though they may be busy.

Mature adults often spend much of their time teaching others. They may still be learning themselves, but it is also time for them to pass on their experience.

Adults often have many other people to think of. Their families and the people they work with need them and take up much of their time and energy.

When people have worked at one job for a long time, they may want to try something entirely new.

Friendship is important to mature adults. They make new friends but keep many old friends, too. They may still have friends from before they started going to school.

Parents can often help their children best by listening to them, as well as telling them what to do. They can learn from their children, too.

Most people enjoy good health all through their adult years. They take care of their bodies by keeping fit, eating well and taking time to relax.

Tasting

Taste is the **sense** that lets you know the flavour of food and drink. The taste of food helps you enjoy eating and drinking. It can also tell you if something has spoiled. Food must be moist to be tasted. Your mouth makes a liquid called saliva, or spit. It mixes with your food as you chew. Once the food is moist it reacts with tiny bumps on your tongue called taste buds. Your taste buds work closely with your smell **detectors** to tell you what is in your mouth.

When you are eating, **chemicals** from the food in your mouth travel up the back of your throat and into your nose. They let you smell the food and help you to recognize its taste. Most of the flavours in food are picked up by the smell detectors in your nose.

Certain tastes are picked up by the taste buds on your tongue and at the back of your throat. There are four kinds of taste buds and each picks up a different flavour.

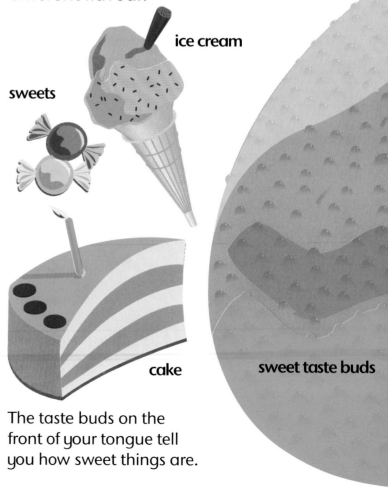

ice cream

sweets

cake

sweet taste buds

▲ Many people and animals like sweet foods. Hummingbirds love nectar, which is many times sweeter than pure sugar.

The taste buds on the front of your tongue tell you how sweet things are.

Taste buds on the sides of your tongue tell you if something is sour.

lemon

lime

At the back of your tongue and in your throat are detectors that pick up bitter tastes. They can warn you not to swallow. Many poisonous plants taste bitter.

dark chocolate

coffee

sour taste buds

bitter taste buds

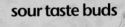

sour taste buds

tongue

salty taste buds

crisps

In the middle of your tongue are taste buds that detect salt. They help to make sure that you eat enough salt. Your body's **cells** need some salt to work properly.

Touching

You use your **sense** of touch to find out how things feel against your skin. When you touch something, or it touches you, tiny **detectors** in your skin send messages to your brain. They tell you about the shape and size of things you touch, and exactly what they feel like, such as rough, smooth, wet or dry.

▼ Touching a special friend or a favourite pet is a good feeling.

Did you know?

You have ticklish places on your skin, such as the bottoms of your feet. When someone touches them, you giggle. Most people do not really like to be tickled, but they almost always laugh.

There are several million points, spread over your whole body, that detect different kinds of touch.

Your body quickly gets used to a touch that stays the same and does not feel uncomfortable. You do not usually feel the touch of your clothes and shoes against your skin. But if they begin to rub or make you feel too hot, your touch detectors soon let you know.

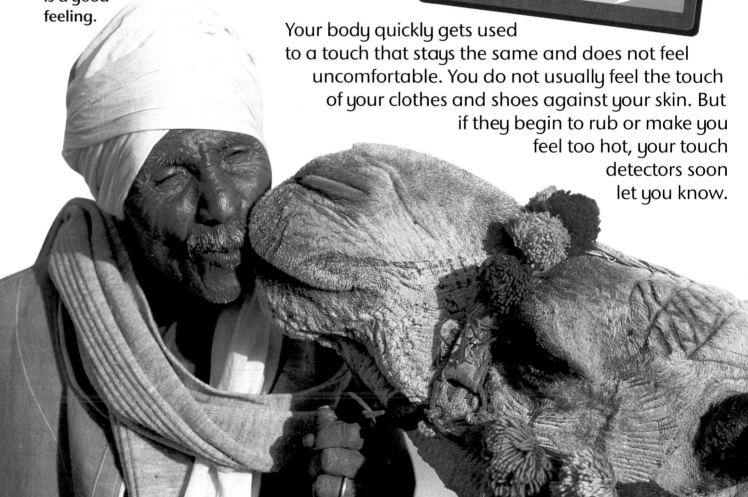

► Some kinds of touch, such as cool water splashing on your skin, can make you shiver.

How does it feel?
Your skin is very good at letting you know when something is soft or hard, hot or cold. When you touch a piece of sandpaper, the detectors in your skin tell your brain that this is a rough object. If you pick up an ice cube, your sense of touch tells you that this object is cold.

You have touch detectors all over, but some parts of your body have more than others. The more detectors your skin contains, the more it can tell you about the thing you are touching. The skin on your back has very few detectors. Your fingertips, tongue and lips have the most.

► Babies often put things into their mouths to find out what they feel like.

Older adults

For older adults, the pace of life may be a little easier than it was in their middle years. If they have children, the children probably have their own homes. Older adults often work less and have more time for themselves, their friends and their families. If they're lucky, they can share their experiences and knowledge of life with others.

Many older adults enjoy making time for grandchildren and other young people they know.

Older people can remember things that happened before you were born. Sometimes they can tell you about your family's history.

Older adults often have the time to be with friends and do exactly as they please, just as they did when they were much younger.

Sometimes older adults may need your help. There is plenty you can do, such as helping around the house and garden.

As their lives become less hectic, many older adults find time for things they couldn't do in younger years.

Voice

Your voice is the sound you make with your throat and mouth. It lets you speak to people and tell them what you think or feel.

❶ When you decide you want to say something, your brain sends messages telling the muscles in your throat and mouth to move.

You can shout loudly enough to be heard from far away, or whisper a secret for only one person to hear. Your voice can also sing, hum, and make a whole range of other sounds just for fun.

❸ As you breathe out, air rushes through the small gap between your vocal cords. This makes them shiver or vibrate, which makes a sound. The sound can change from a deep murmur to a high squeak when your vocal cords move.

❷ There are two flaps in your throat, rather like pieces of skin. These are your vocal cords. They move together so that your throat partly closes.

vocal cords

The way we use our voices to speak to each other is one of the main things that makes people different from other animals. But people who can't use their vocal cords can still talk to one another. They use their hands to make signs.

▶ Babies learn the meaning of the sounds other people make. Then they learn to use their own voices to make sounds that others can understand.

Mouth sounds

Some sounds are made by your lips and tongue. You can change a sound by moving your mouth in different ways.

o

a

e

Your voice is not just for telling people things. It is a kind of musical instrument, too. By varying the **pitch** of noises between high and low, you can make the sound of a tune. Singing is a talking tune.

Your voice changes as you get older. Around the age of 12, a boy's voice becomes deeper. His vocal cords grow which changes the pitch of the sounds he makes as he speaks. A girl's voice deepens a little as she gets older, but this happens very gradually.

Glossary

Biological Your mother and father, who passed on their **genes** to you when you were born, are your biological parents.

Calcium A soft, white, stony mineral.

Capillaries Tiny tubes inside your body which carry blood between your bigger veins and arteries.

Carbohydrate A **substance** found in foods such as bread, which gives you **energy**.

Carbon dioxide A **gas** which is found in the air that you breathe out from your lungs.

Cells The smallest parts of an animal or plant. Your body is made up of many millions of cells.

Chemical A solid, liquid or **gas** that can act and react with other **substances**.

Detector A part of your body which picks up information from the world around you.

Digest To break down food inside your body, so that the **nutrients** and **energy** from the food can be used by your different body parts.

Digestive system All the parts of your body, from your mouth to your intestine, which work to **digest** your food.

Energy What makes people able to live and do work. Your energy comes from the food you eat.

Flexible Able to bend easily without breaking.

Focus To bring light **rays** together, so that they meet and make a clear picture.

Fraternal Twins who do not share the same genes and do not look exactly alike.

Gas A **substance**, such as air, which is not solid or liquid. Most gases are light and float above the ground.

Gene Part of your **cells** which comes from your parents and controls what your body is like and the way you look.

Germ A tiny living thing that can make people sick.

Gland A part of your body which makes the **chemicals** you need to keep your body working.

Material A **substance**, either natural or made by people, which in turn is often used to make other things.

Microscope A tool which lets you see something very small by making it look bigger.

Mucus A slimy, wet **substance** made by some parts of your body, such as your nose.

Nerve A bundle of living fibres that carries messages between your brain and your body.

Nutrients The **substances** in food which your body uses to grow.

Oxygen A **gas** with no colour or smell that is found in the air. All animals and plants need oxygen to live.

Pitch How high or low a sound is.

Protect To keep something or someone safe from harm.

Protein Something that is found in all living cells of plants and animals. We eat protein in foods such as meat, milk and beans.

Ray A beam of light.

Sense How living things know about their surroundings and their own bodies. People have the sense of seeing, hearing, smelling, touching and tasting.

Skeleton The bony frame that **protects** and holds up the body of an animal.

Substance What something is made from. Solids, liquids and gases are all substances.

Temperature How hot or cold something is.

Waste Something which has been used and is no longer needed, or something which is left over from a process.

Index